SCIENCE SECRETS

Written by Robyn Supraner
Illustrated by Renzo Barto

Troll Associates

Library of Congress Cataloging in Publication Data

Supraner, Robyn.
    Science Secrets.
    SUMMARY: Instructions for doing simple experiments
which prove basic scientific principles.
    1. Science—Experiments—Juvenile literature.
[1. Science—Experiments.   2. Experiments]   I. Barto,
Renzo.   II. Title.
Q164.S87   507′.8   80-23794
ISBN 0-89375-426-9
ISBN 0-89375-427-7 (pbk.)

CONTENTS

NO ROOM! NO ROOM!

Here's what you need:

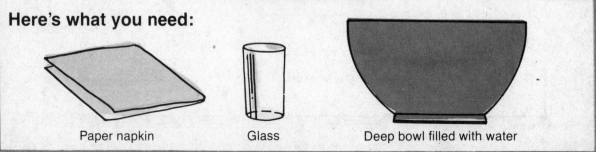

Paper napkin   Glass   Deep bowl filled with water

Here's what you do:

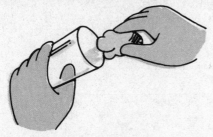

1 Crumple a paper napkin and push it to the bottom of a glass.

2 Fill a deep bowl with enough water to cover the glass.

3 Turn the glass upside down and push it straight into the water. Don't tip the glass!

4 Now, without tipping it, quickly pull the glass out of the water.

5 Take out the napkin. What happened? The napkin stayed dry!

Here's why: When you push the glass into the water, air gets trapped inside the glass. The air takes up all the empty space. There is no room for the water to get in. Try the experiment again. This time, tip the glass. What happens? Why?

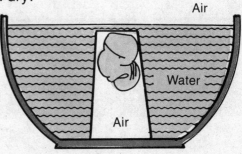

THE MAGIC BOTTLE

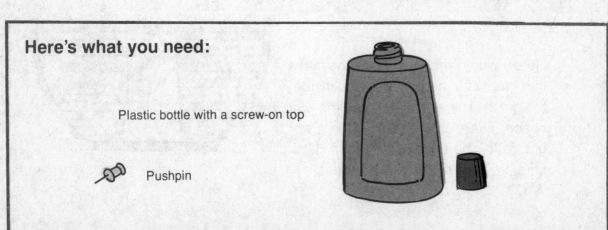

Here's what you need:

Plastic bottle with a screw-on top

Pushpin

Here's what you do:

1 Poke a small hole in the side of a plastic bottle with a pushpin. Leave the pin in place.

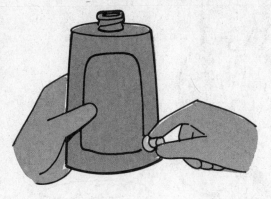

2 Press your thumb against the pushpin. Fill the bottle with water. Fill it to the very top.

3 Screw on the top.

4 Now, remove the pushpin. The water does not pour out of the hole! It stays in the bottle.

Here's why: Water pushes from inside the bottle. Air presses from outside the bottle. The air presses harder than the water in the bottle. Air pressure keeps the water from pouring out.

If you tell your friends it's magic, don't forget to say *abracadabra!*

THE TOOTHPICK TRICK

All things are made up of many tiny particles. These particles are called *molecules.* Molecules of water tend to stick together.

Here's what you need:

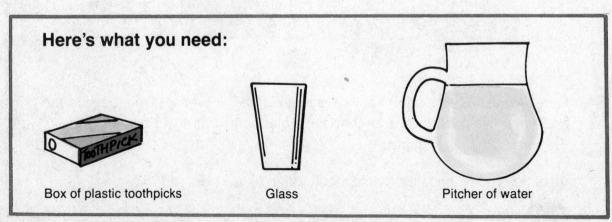

Box of plastic toothpicks   Glass   Pitcher of water

Here's what you do:

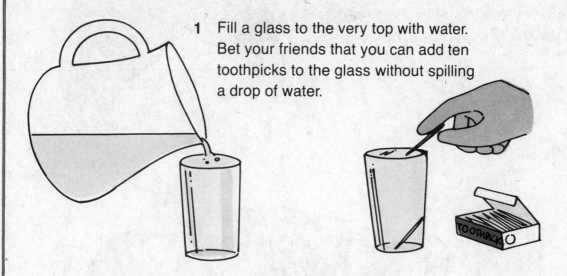

1 Fill a glass to the very top with water. Bet your friends that you can add ten toothpicks to the glass without spilling a drop of water.

2 Drop the toothpicks into the glass, one at a time. (*Note:* Count out loud as you do this. It makes the trick more dramatic!)

3 When you have added the ten toothpicks, smile sweetly at your audience. Then add ten more toothpicks! Do this very carefully. The water will bulge above the top of the glass, but it will not spill over.

This is why: The molecules of water stick to each other. They form an invisible "skin" that holds the water together. If you add enough toothpicks, the "skin" will break, and the water will spill. How many toothpicks can you add without spilling the water?

HOW FULL IS FULL?

A cup is filled with boiling water.
Is it really full?

Here's what you need:

Spoon

Sugar

Measuring cup

Pot holder

Kettle of water

Here's what you do:

1 Boil some water. (*Note:* If you are not allowed to use the stove by yourself, ask a grownup for help.)

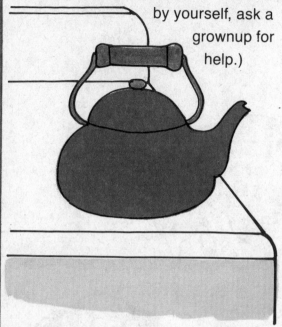

2 Pour the boiling water into a measuring cup. *Remember to use a pot holder!* Fill the cup to the very top.

3 Sprinkle a spoonful of sugar into the boiling water. Then add another spoonful. And another.

4 The sugar disappears, but the water does not rise. Where does the sugar go? There are tiny pockets of air among the molecules of water.

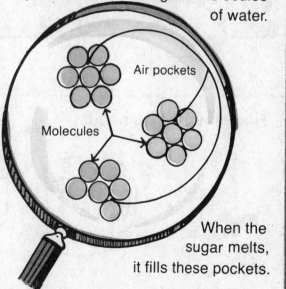

Air pockets

Molecules

When the sugar melts, it fills these pockets.

COME BACK, SUGAR!

You have seen that sugar disappears in boiling water. But is it gone forever?

Here's what you need:

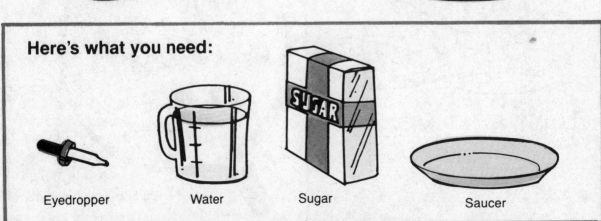

Eyedropper   Water   Sugar   Saucer

Here's what you do:

1 Fill an eyedropper with sugar water.

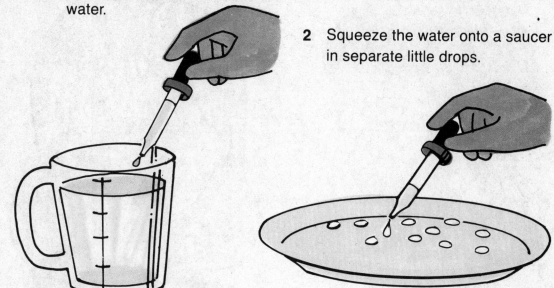

2 Squeeze the water onto a saucer in separate little drops.

3 Place the saucer in the sun or under a lamp.

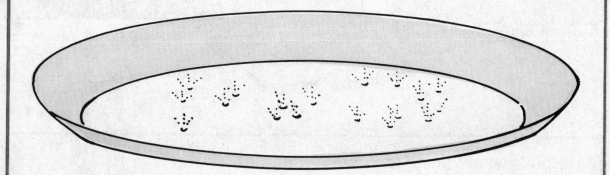

When the water has dried up, look closely at the saucer. You will find white sugar crystals where the droplets used to be! Try this experiment with tea or coffee. What is left when the water evaporates?

WILL IT OR WON'T IT?

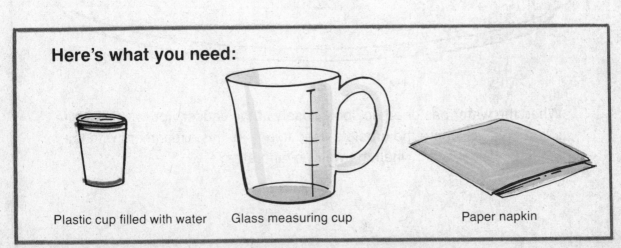

Here's what you need:

Plastic cup filled with water   Glass measuring cup   Paper napkin

Here's what you do:

1 Put the plastic cup, filled with water, into the freezer. After the water is frozen solid, run warm water over the outside of the cup. This will loosen the ice from the cup.

2 Place the ice in the measuring cup.

3 Fill the cup with warm water. Fill it to the very top. The ice will float. Some of the ice will stick out of the water.

4 Put the cup on the napkin. What will happen when the ice melts? Will all the water fit in the cup? Or will some spill over onto the napkin? Will it or won't it?

5 Wait for the ice to melt. Then look at the napkin. It will be dry. When the water was frozen, it did not fit in the cup. But the melted water did fit. Here's why: Water takes up more space when it is frozen.

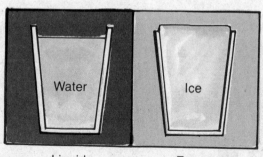

Liquid   Frozen

Extra: Push the floating ice down into the water. It will pop right up again. That's because ice is lighter than water.

MUSICAL BOTTLES

Here's what you need:

4 Bottles, all of the same size and shape, and some water

Here's what you do:

1 Fill the first bottle with water. Put less water in the second bottle. Put even less water in the third bottle. Leave the fourth bottle empty.

2 Blow across the top of each bottle. Each sounds different than the others! The more water in the bottle, the higher the sound the bottle makes. Can you play a song on your musical bottles?

Here's why: When you blow across the tops of the bottles, it causes the air in each bottle to vibrate. These vibrations make sound. Each bottle has a different amount of air in it, so the sound it makes is different than the other bottles.

THE MYSTERY OF THE CROOKED BEAN SPROUT

The stem of a plant grows straight up, and its roots grow straight down. You can prove it by making them grow crooked!

Here's what you need:

Dried bean   Paper towel   Glass

Here's what you do:

1 Wet a paper towel.

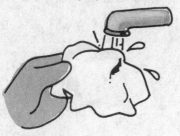

2 Squeeze out most of the water.

3 Stuff the towel into a clear glass.

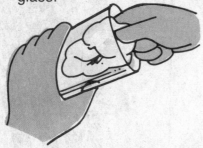

4 Tuck a dried bean between the folds of the towel. Place the bean where you can see it.

5 Rest the glass on its side. Each day, sprinkle the paper towel with water. Soon the bean will send out roots and then a stem. The stem will grow upward. The roots will grow downward.

6 When the stem has grown about an inch, stand the glass up straight.

7 Continue to sprinkle the towel with water. As the bean sprout grows, its stem and roots will change direction. Again, the stem will grow straight up! Again, the roots will grow straight down!

LOVE THAT CHAIR!

Here's what you need:

A chair   A wall   A friend

Here's what you do:

1   Place a chair about 18 inches from the wall.

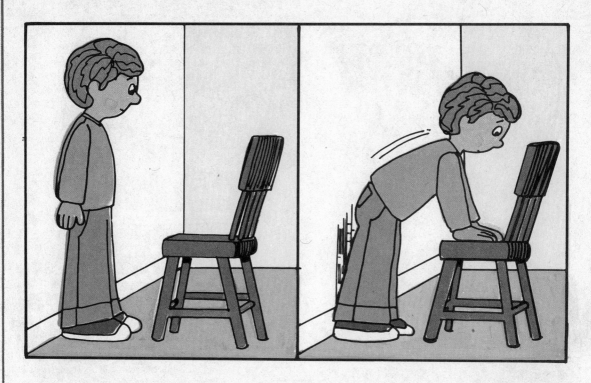

2   Ask a friend to stand between the chair and the wall. Tell him to bend over and rest his hands on the seat of the chair.

3   Now tell him to place his heels against the wall and say, as loudly as he can, *"Love that chair!"*.

4   Your friend will not be able to let go of the chair. Tell him if he lets go for even a second, the chair will pull him back!

Here's why: The earth is a giant magnet. Its magnetic force is called *gravity*. Gravity pulls things down. It is pulling your friend down because he is off balance. Without a center of balance, he cannot fight the pull of gravity.

PAPER WORM

When is a straw wrapper like a worm?
When it wiggles!

Here's what you need:

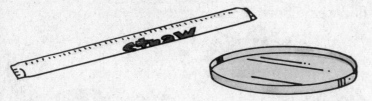

Straw in its paper wrapper

Plate or plastic lid

Water

Here's what you do:

1 Hold the wrapped straw in your hand and push the wrapper down to one end of the straw.

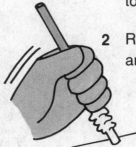

2 Remove the crumpled wrapper and put it on a plate or plastic lid.

3 Sprinkle the wrapper with a drop or two of water.

4 Watch the paper wrapper stretch and wiggle like a worm.

Here's why: The wrapper swells as it absorbs the drops of water. As it swells, the paper straightens out, moving and wiggling like a worm.

THE WISE KING

A very wise king was asked to decide which of two apples was bigger. The red one was fatter. The green one was taller. But which one was bigger? Which took up more space? All the king had was a bowl of water and a crayon. Can you guess what he did?

Here's what you need:

2 Apples

Bowl of water

Crayon

Here's what you do:

1   Place one of the apples in a bowl of water. Be sure the apple is completely covered with water.

2   On the inside of the bowl, mark the level of the water with a crayon.

3   Remove the apple.

4   Place the other apple in the bowl of water. Again, mark the level of the water.

5   Remove the second apple.

6   Compare the crayon marks. Which one is higher? The higher the mark, the bigger the apple!

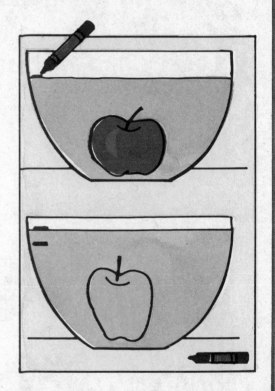

Here's why: The bigger apple displaces more water. It pushes more water up and out of the way and takes its place. What else can you measure this way? Why not see who has the biggest hand?

THE WISE QUEEN

A wise queen was asked to pick up an apple without touching it with any part of her body. She could, if she liked, use a drinking straw.

"No problem," said the queen, and she proceeded to pick up the apple! You can do it too.

Here's what you need:

Drinking straw   Apple

Here's what you do:

1 Put an apple on the kitchen counter.

2 Hold it steady with one hand.

3 Hold the straw with four fingers wrapped around it and your thumb placed firmly on top.

4 Hold the straw above the apple as straight as you can.

5 Then quickly push the straw into the apple. (*Hint:* Hold the straw close to the apple. When you push, push hard. You may break a few straws at first but keep trying. It really works!)

6 Pick up the apple with the straw. You are not touching it with any part of your body.

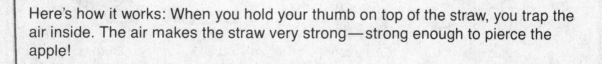

Here's how it works: When you hold your thumb on top of the straw, you trap the air inside. The air makes the straw very strong—strong enough to pierce the apple!

STAR SHINER

When you get to know the stars, you will be able to find wonderful pictures in the night sky.

Here's what you need:

| Hammer | Empty can | Nail | Crayon | Flashlight |

Here's what you do:

1 Remove the top of an empty can, and turn the can upside down.

2 Draw one of these constellations on the bottom of the can with a crayon.

(*Note:* A constellation is a group of stars. It forms a shape, or picture, in the sky. Each constellation has a special name.)

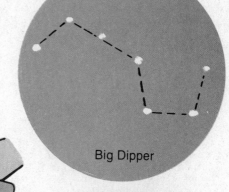

Big Dipper

3 Mark the place where each star goes.

4 With a hammer and nail, make a hole for each star.

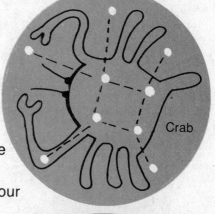

Crab

5 Take your Star Shiner into a dark room. Shine a flashlight into the Star Shiner, so the light shines on the ceiling. The points of light on your ceiling will look like the stars in the sky.

Extra: Make other constellations. Label each can, so you will remember the names of the constellations. Have a "sky show" with your friends. Arrange the constellations on your ceiling the way they appear in the sky.

Gaze at the sky some starry night. How many constellations can you find?

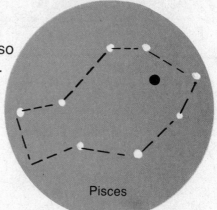

Pisces

LAZY NEWSPAPER

Tell your friends that you have some very lazy newspapers. Then prove it!

Here's what you need:

Ruler

Newspaper

Here's what you do:

1 Place a ruler on a table. Make sure part of it sticks out over the edge of the table.

2 Cover the part of the ruler that is on the table with a few sheets of newspaper. Overlap the newspaper and smooth it down, so the sheets lie flat.

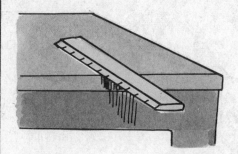

(*Note:* The edge of the newspaper should lie along the edge of the table.)

3 Now ask your friends to move the newspaper by striking the end of the ruler. They will be surprised when the paper refuses to move no matter how hard they try!

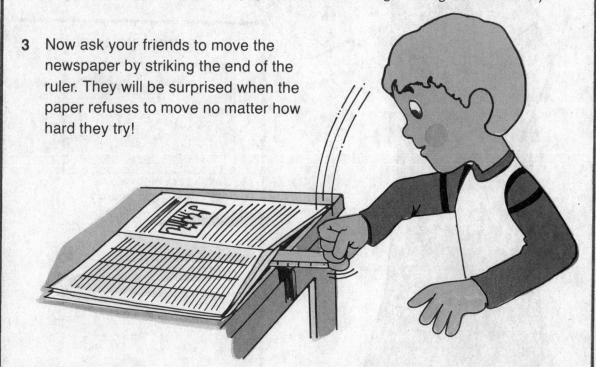

Here's why: The newspaper is at rest. A thing at rest tends to stay that way. It resists movement. The harder you try to move it, the more it resists. The way to move the newspaper is to press down on the stick very, very slowly!

GRAVITY FIGHTER

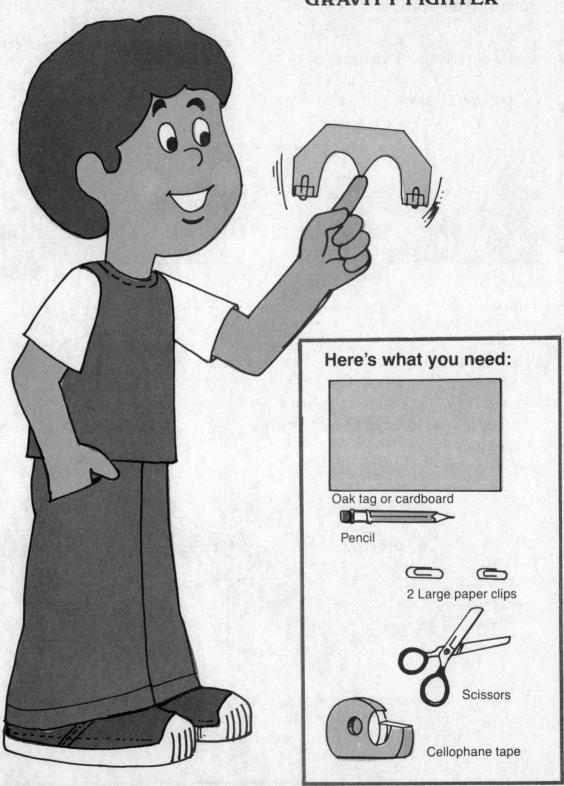

Here's what you need:

Oak tag or cardboard

Pencil

2 Large paper clips

Scissors

Cellophane tape

Here's what you do:

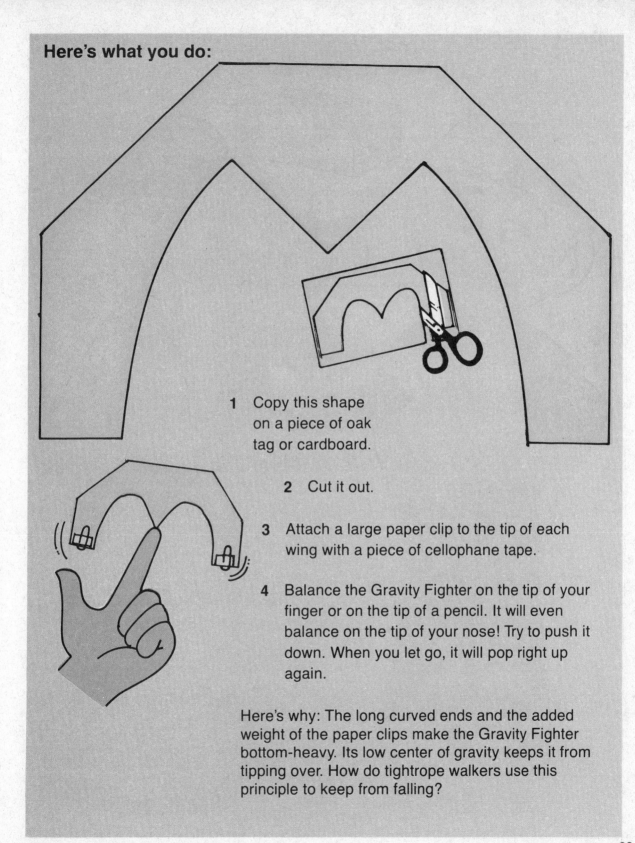

1 Copy this shape on a piece of oak tag or cardboard.

2 Cut it out.

3 Attach a large paper clip to the tip of each wing with a piece of cellophane tape.

4 Balance the Gravity Fighter on the tip of your finger or on the tip of a pencil. It will even balance on the tip of your nose! Try to push it down. When you let go, it will pop right up again.

Here's why: The long curved ends and the added weight of the paper clips make the Gravity Fighter bottom-heavy. Its low center of gravity keeps it from tipping over. How do tightrope walkers use this principle to keep from falling?

DAFFY DECK!

Here's what you need:

Shoe box

Deck of playing cards

Here's what you do:

1 Place an empty shoe box on the floor in front of you.

2 Hold a playing card between your thumb and index finger.

3 Stand up straight and drop the card into the shoe box. If you miss, try again.

4 You will be puzzled to see each card sail away, just as it is about to fall into the box!

Here's why: Air currents form as the card is falling. Air pressure forces the card to swerve as it nears the box.

Solution:

Do not stand directly in front of the box. Stand over to one side. Before you drop the card, slightly tilt the bottom of it toward the box. (This controls the air pressure.) When the card swerves, it will land in the box!

HUMMINGBIRD

Here's what you need:

A friend who is a good sport

Here's what you do:

1 Ask a friend to hum a song. His mouth must be kept closed while humming.

2 Bet him that you can make him stop humming by touching him with two fingers. If he looks suspicious, promise it won't hurt.

3 While he is humming, gently pinch his nose. He will not be able to hum another note!

Here's why: Humming sounds are made by air passing over your vocal cords. When your air supply is cut off, you cannot make a sound. Hold your hand against the front of your throat. Now hum. Can you feel the vibration of your vocal cords?

How can you get a hummingbird to stop humming? Teach it the words.

FUN WITH MAGNETS

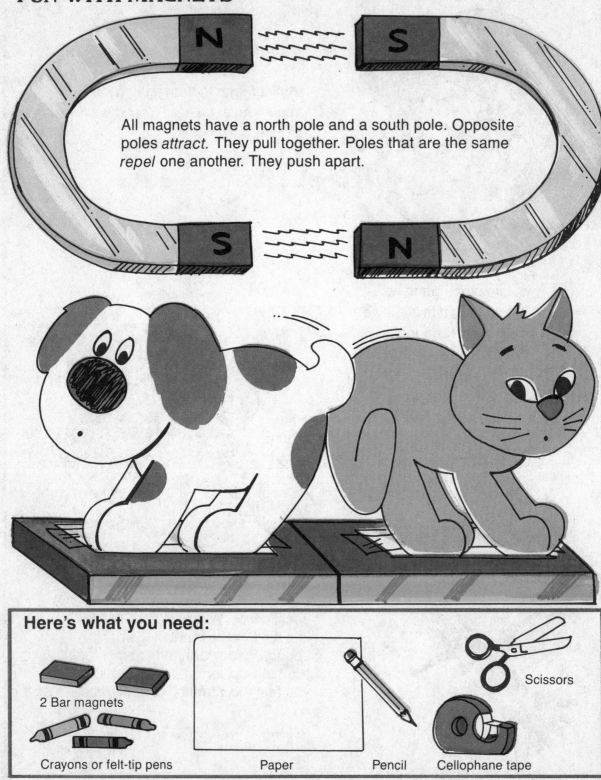

All magnets have a north pole and a south pole. Opposite poles *attract*. They pull together. Poles that are the same *repel* one another. They push apart.

Here's what you need:

2 Bar magnets

Crayons or felt-tip pens

Paper

Pencil

Scissors

Cellophane tape

Here's what you do:

1 Draw a cat and a dog on a piece of paper. Add tabs below their feet as shown.

2 Color the animals and cut them out.

3 Fold the tabs along the dotted line.

4 Tape each figure to a bar magnet. Now, use what you know about magnets to make the dog chase the cat. Make the cat chase the dog. Can you get them to kiss and make up?

Extra: Place the cat and the dog on a glass table or on a piece of cardboard. Control their movements with a nail held underneath the table.

MAKE YOUR OWN MAGNET

Here's what you need:

Paper clip   Nail   Bar magnet

Here's what you do:

1 Rub a nail across a bar magnet about 30 to 35 times. Rub it in one direction only. Do *not* rub it back and forth!

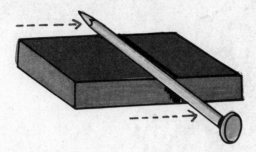

2 Hold the nail near the paper clip. If the paper clip jumps up to meet the nail, the nail has been magnetized. If it does not, rub the nail against the magnet some more.

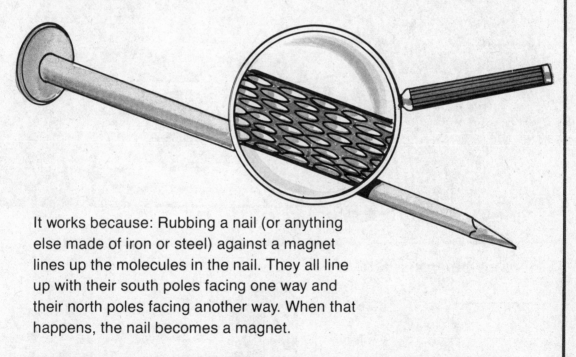

It works because: Rubbing a nail (or anything else made of iron or steel) against a magnet lines up the molecules in the nail. They all line up with their south poles facing one way and their north poles facing another way. When that happens, the nail becomes a magnet.

Extra: To take away the nail's magnetic power, throw it on the ground as hard as you can! This disturbs the lines of molecules. When they are no longer lined up, the nail cannot act as a magnet.

INVISIBLE INK

Here's what you need:

Paper　　　Small glass　　　Milk or lemon juice　　　Iron

Toothpick

MILK

Here's what you do:

1 Pour some milk or lemon juice into a small glass.

2 Write a message on a piece of paper. Use the lemon juice or the milk for ink. Use a toothpick for a pen.

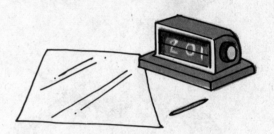

3 Wait for the "ink" to dry. Your message will be invisible.

4 Run a heated iron over the paper a few times. (*Note:* If you are not allowed to use an iron by yourself, ask a grownup for help.) After a while, your message will mysteriously appear!

Here's why: Some things burn more easily than others. When milk or lemon juice are dry, they burn more easily than paper.

This is a good way to write a secret message to a friend!

THE COLOR MIXER

Here's what you need:

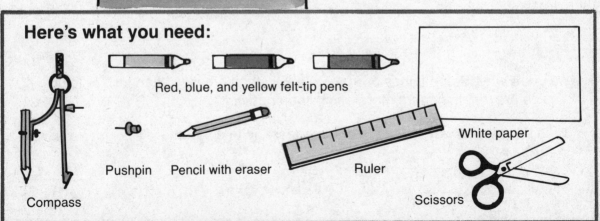

Red, blue, and yellow felt-tip pens

Compass

Pushpin   Pencil with eraser   Ruler

White paper

Scissors

44

Here's what you do:

1   Use a compass to draw a 4-inch circle on a piece of white paper. Cut the circle out.

2   Inside the circle, draw a 2-inch circle and 3-inch circle.

3   Use a ruler to divide the circle into 6 parts as shown.

4   Color the sections red, blue, and yellow. These are the *primary* colors. Follow the pattern shown here.

5   Stick a pushpin through the center of the circle and into the eraser tip of a pencil.

6   Hold the pencil in one hand. With your other hand, spin the circle as fast as you can. Watch the colors change from red, blue, and yellow to orange, purple, and green. These are the *secondary* colors.

Here's why: The disk spins so fast that your eyes "mix" the colors together. You see them as a combination of the three primary colors.

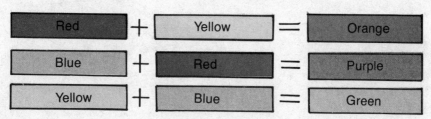

Red	+	Yellow	=	Orange
Blue	+	Red	=	Purple
Yellow	+	Blue	=	Green

AIR POWER

Here's what you need:

Balloon

Large book

Here's what you do:

1 Announce to your friends that you will attempt to raise a heavy book into the air without touching it.

2 Then place a balloon on a table. The balloon's opening should be hanging off the edge of the table.

3 Place a heavy book on top of the balloon.

4 Take a deep breath and blow steadily into the balloon. You will surprise everyone with how easily the book is raised into the air.

Here's what happens: Air under pressure can be used to move objects that are too heavy to be moved by hand.